About the Author

Gilli Bloodaxe is an English poet from the north (1955 – 2037 based on current projections). He writes and performs in clubs, in crypts, on barges, on buses, by the sea strand and at festivals like Latitude, Beautiful Days, Ambition and Brighton Festival Fringe. His work has appeared on BBC Radio 3's Late Junction, Stuart Maconie's Freakier Zone (BBC Radio 6), BBC Radio 3's The Verb and on Radio Resonance FM. This is his first collection of poetry. Under a ridiculous pseudonym, he has also played many gigs and festivals as a flamenco guitarist and drummer.

www.gillibloodaxe.co.uk

To Marie. Hope you enjoy it! Lots of love

Bloodaxe

FIN

A COLLECTION OF POEMS

ILLUSTRATED BY
LILY MORGAN

GILLI BLOODAXE

EDITED BY CLARE GILL

Matador
9 Priory Business Park,
Wistow Road, Kibworth Beauchamp,
Leicestershire. LE8 0RX
Tel: (+44) 116 279 2299
Email: books@troubador.co.uk
Web: www.troubador.co.uk/matador

ISBN 978 1784624 804

British Library Cataloguing in Publication Data.
A catalogue record for this book is available from the British Library.

Printed and bound in the UK by TJ International, Padstow, Cornwall
Typeset in 11pt Aldine BTRoman by Troubador Publishing Ltd, Leicester, UK

Matador is an imprint of Troubador Publishing Ltd

Dedicated to Judy Winter – best of friends

Silver and Red

Granny mistrusted nurses and docs,
so turned to traditional remedies when
she caught the pox
off my Uncle Ken.

She heard that in bygone days
mercury was taken for clap,
so she scoured the car boots under gunmetal grey,
picking through all the crap.

All the thermometers she could find
she emptied into a pot,
and from that quicksilver she'd combined
she'd take a daily tot.

She also took a dose
in her Ovaltine at night.
Now here's where things get gross
and granny gets a **FRIGHT**

Over a month or two
the colour of her skin
changed, it itched, then, euw!
dropped
      off.
Her cheeky grin

distorted as her t$_e$e$_t$h
fell out, then her n$_a$i$_l$s,
then her barnet. When she
walked by she left a trail l l l ı ı ı ı ı ı

She sweated, salivated,
pissed needles and pins
and though the pain abated
she suffered for her sins.

There was life in the old dog yet,
and her figure looked just great,
but all the mercury that she ate
began to accumulate.

Of course, she passed away,
but not from the toxin.
She won a bungee jump in Take a Break
from colouring Jamie Foxx in.

She made her way to a high location.
Bungeeman clocked her slim physique
and did the calculations.
Off she leapt with an awful   s
                                   h
                                   r
                                   i
                                   e
                                   k.

Granny, plus a few stone
of mercury, dropped like lead
and landed in an abstract of bone
and silver and red.

Zodiac

Aquarius: You will unexpectedly find a biscuit.
Pisces: You will have sex but wonder why.
Aries: Your loved ones will abandon you.
Taurus: You will feel a bit funny.
Gemini: You will lose your faith in God.
Cancer: You will play football with some ladies.
Leo: You will vary your punctuation?
Virgo: You will find yourself in Barrow-in-Furness.
Libra: You will see your future and die from despair.
Scorpio: You will go to the toilet carelessly.
Sagittarius: Though no-one rings the doorbell, you
will answer the door then run away.
Capricorn: You will be wrongly diagnosed with
hypochondria.

Apparently, my horoscope said
"Today you will win one hundred pounds."
I didn't believe in astrology
so I didn't read the horoscope
but I did win one hundred pounds.
Now I do believe in astrology
but because I am superstitious,
I still won't read my horoscope.

I was born on the 5th day
of May
1955.
I went to the track, and arrived
to see that in the 5th race,
at 5 o'clock, was a horse called Pentagon Place.
At the ATM I found
I had £555 in my account.
I took it out and said "Put it on Pentagon herewith."
It came 5th.
Ha ha ha ha ha.

(Poem as) Garden (as Poem)

And and and
And and and

Grubbing around the veg patch
sun pink smarting bald patch,
disturbing deep dank smells of decay
and soil and mould and and and.
Everything changes,
brown to green,
hidden, exposed,
hingebonecoinflintglassshard.
Dead to living
as the compost bins alchemically
transform base peelings into
gold black nutty humus.
Living to dead,
the involuntary soft explosion
of caracoles downtrodden.
Nothing changes.
That fence post is rotten.

No bad workman, I clean and and and praise my
tools, like me, from Sheffield.

Like a poem, everything's there,
just needs licking into shape -
change this,
prune that,
discard here,
transplant there.

Shed door's jamming.

Edward's Shed

Edward de Bono went to B&Q to buy a shed.
It was delivered to his house within 14 working days,
but when Edward laid it out on the lawn, to his dismay
he saw that pieces of shed – he'd plenty;
the instructions – he had nanty.
Anyone else whose shed was thus tainted
would have gone back to the shop to get reacquainted
with the salesman, but Edward was lateral –
rather than cackle and chatter, all
he wanted was to kick off his sneakers
and come up with a solution. Eureka!
He trolled round to the corner shop and bought up all
their stock of bungees
and a couple of Crunchies.
He built a matrix of cords
connecting the roof to the floor,
and each wall to its opposite wall.
Though it shook ⁽⁽⁽back⁾⁾⁾ and ⁽⁽⁽fro⁾⁾⁾
when it started to blow,
the shed was as sound as a pound.
As he went back to the house – the door bell! - ♫
and through the fenestra – bloody hell! -

he saw the uniform, not of Plod,
but the TV licence detective squad.
Without thinking, down the garden he fled,
looking for sanctuary, and ran into his shed.
The matrix of bungees yielded, then
flung him   ((((((back up the garden
into the luppers of Hector,
the surprised detector,
who had not even come about his telly – oh no! -
but to j^{igg}le the willets of Mrs De Bono.

The Curve of Your Neck

The curve of your neck,
the smell of your hair,
the feel of your skin.

I really miss you grandad.

They found him dead at the bottom of the stairs.
It seems that he didn't fall,
but was sliding down the bannisters naked
when his pubic hair snagged on a spindle,
and the pain caused his heart to fail.
My grandmother, also naked and close behind,
fell on top and finished him off.

It's how he would have wanted to go.

Pussy Sandwich Gliders

I planted a pippin pip in 2003.
It grew with love and care
and though no fruit did it bear,
I loved my little apple tree.

One day as I strode forth
I saw my tree was gone.
I told my neighbour, John,
and we looked down at the earth.

On local trees I'd seen adverts, or
notices for lost putty tats.
And if trees could be used for cats,
why not vicey versa?

I clipped an open ring binder
on a moggy's back and made a sort
of little sandwich board
on which to seek a finder.

**"LOST, LITTLE APPLE TREE
(MALUS DOMESTICA) OVAL LEAVES"**
and, hoping to engage the thieves,
a photo for all to see,

of the tree, behind my brother Ken.
I clipped binders on all the cats I could
and I really absolutely should
have foreseen what happened then.

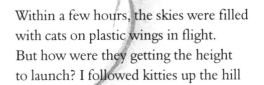

Within a few hours, the skies were filled
with cats on plastic wings in flight.
But how were they getting the height
to launch? I followed kitties up the hill

and watched as they cut round the fence
of grumpy Mr Guest who lived at The Crest.
They climbed my little tree, looked west
and launched themselves hence.

Now rotten Mr Guest is inside, the
tree stealer ensnared,
his crimes laid bare
by the pussy sandwich gliders.

Farming Today

Danty sits at the bleached table
with the deep, rabbit-chopped valleys
in silence.
The radio, low of battery, weak of signal,
twists and buckles Farming Today, nagging
"Get your gansy on and do some work."
His dry stone face takes cover
beneath hair swept across like yonsycamores
blasted sideways by the wind
and the 12 bore pellets shot at Turk's head crows.

Danty peers through the muck and weed-blinded window
(contrast the arse of his trousers,
lustrous as the Duchess's mirror)
peers down the deep, rabbit-hopped gills,
sheep velcroed to the sheer sides.

Danty, unvisited since the business with the pig's head,
that was only a bloody joke!
From this house full of unpairs –
pestle, cup, dustpan, mop –
himself unpaired twenty years since,
neither church bells nor Six Bells draw him.

He looses the latch and out he clomps.
Above his head, the sky splits open.

Hoot

The kids loved it when Uncle Dwight came
walking down the street.
He always brought them sweets
and thought up funny games.

"Uncle Dwight, what shall we play today?"
"Today's game is of dressing up.
Now listen you young pups,
here's how you play...

you wait in the bedroom
and tightly close your eyes.
I'll go down and get disguised.
After five minutes, you come

down and guess my game."
After five minutes giggling they ran
downstairs to find a masked man
removing art from frames.

The kids squealed with glee.
"You're a burglar, Uncle Dwight!"
The masked man said "That's right
children, now hold the door for me

while I load this into my truck."
As they waved him off
down the street, a cough
from the dining room and a suck

of breath were all
that could be heard.
Things went blurred
for Dwight, curled in a ball

no air inside his astronaut suit.
And as he passed away
he could be heard to say
"What a lark, eh, kids, what a hoot!"

No id, no sale

I went down the offie for some ale
and saw this sign:

No id, no sale.

But without an id, which Sigmund Freud described as the
source of our bodily needs, impulses, desires, and wants,
I wouldn't have fancied a brown bottle in the first place and
drifted into the shop with my usual nonchalance.
To the shopkeeper I said
"It might make more sense if it read
No super-ego, no sale."
But he called me a twat and a failure
and banned me.
Now my choice of off-licences is down from four
to three.

Hi Ho, Bambolini

Network Rail passenger information:
*"Due to a racketeering Turk at Hassocks Station
a replacement bus service is in operation."*

Hi Ho, Bambolini.
Fucking hell, Mussolini
ran the trains on time
but not the Brighton line.

Network Rail passenger information:
*"Due to jissom in the bus carburation
a replacement rickshaw service is in operation."*

Hi Ho, Bambolini.
Fucking hell, Mussolini
ran the trains on time
but not the Brighton line.

Network Rail passenger information:
*"Due to rickshaw wallah's palpitations
a replacement goat-cart service is in operation."*

Hi Ho, Bambolini.
Fucking hell, Mussolini
ran the trains on time
but not the Brighton line.

Network Rail passenger information:
"Due to the goat's excretive ruminations
a replacement pushbike service is in operation."

Hi Ho, Bambolini.
Fucking hell, Mussolini
ran the trains on time
but not the Brighton line.

Network Rail passenger information:
"Due to sick lickle tyre deflation
a replacement pedestrian footway is in operation."

Hi Ho, Bambolini.
Fucking hell, Mussolini
ran the trains on time
but not the Brighton line.

"Victoria, your next station stop is Victoria.
The train now lounging fecklessly at platform 13
is the last train back to Brighton.
Due to an interfering jerk at Hassocks Station
a replacement bus service is in operation…"

Caravaggio

Caravaggio
put his car in the garaggio.
The old master
had painted a go-faster
stripe in ciaraoscuro.
His mate Arturo
said the light and the shade
and the way it was sprayed
made the stripe come to life.
Caravaggio's wife
was less than impressed,
thought it tacky at best,
and went off with Van Dyck
on the back of his bike.

Eureka!

In 250 BC in Syracuse, Archimedes
discovered that when he sat in the bath
he displaced the same amount of water as his body mass.
$$F = Vg \, (\varrho f - \rho 0)$$

Panther, the boxer in the gaff
                                   downstairs
discovered that the mosaic artist Plato,
who did Archimedes' bathroom styling,
had skimped on the tiling.

Whether he ran out of tiles, or ran out of time
or just lost interest, we can't divine,
but Panther had this sneaking feeling
that water was pissing through his ceiling.

It raised his hackles,
and he stormed round to tackle
Plato, ignoring his begs
for mercy. The number of toothiepegs
Panther displaced with the smack in the jaw,
was the same as there were tiles missing from the floor.

"Eureka!" Plato shouted,
as blood spouted
onto the freshly grouted…

In Memoriam

This stone is in memory of Sid Bianca,
keen golfer and total wanker,
who swaggered about this golf course
and bragged about his house and horse
in his slacks of plaid
and his Tiger Woods hat
and his, whatever, poncey car.
But one day he went too far
when he waylaid a wayfarer
already having a mare of a day,
who pulled out Sid's putter
and shoved it up his shutter.
The walker was, I hasten
to add, a stone mason,
and twelve years clink
gave him time to think,
and to carve this
stone. Upon which, feel free to take a piss
and remember Sid
and what he did.

```
┌─────────────────────────┐
│        A q u i          │
│                         │
│        v i v e          │
│                         │
│      u n   p o e t a    │
└─────────────────────────┘
```

Dick gifted me this tile
tongue in cheek.
I stuck it out front
and inside a week
I'd been robbed twice.
"A Poet Lives Here"
it seems, is a warning that
burglars don't fear.

In fact it provokes
the opposite response
to **"Beware Of The Dog"**.
No self-respecting nonce
will be threatened by
an effete floppy fringe
with a velvet jacket
who looks slightly unhinged,
spouts quatrains
then has an asthma attack.

So Dick, tongue in cheek mate,
thanks for the plaque.

(Still, it's good to see that local tea leaves, with their
emotional bandages
have a good working knowledge of modern foreign
languages.)

Seven Poets (1)

Seven poets had a brawl,
man, you shoulda seen 'em.
None of them was hurt at all -
didn't have a punch between 'em.

Seven Poets (2)

Seven poets jumped off a bridge with some ferocity.
They soon reached terminal velocity,
but despite that,
none had time
to find a rhyme
for **splat**.

Russian Dolls

I went to the BBC shop to buy
a present for my Aunty Vi.
They had a set of Russian dolls,
but instead of being Russian, or dolls,
or any women wearing cardies,
they were models of the Doctor's Tardis.
I opened the first one, and found a smaller one inside.
I opened it, and found a smaller one inside.
I opened it, and found a smaller one inside.
I opened it, and found a smaller one inside.
I opened it, and found a smaller one inside.

Eventually I came to the last one.
I knew it was the last one,
because inside, it was much bigger than the previous one.
I opened it, and found a bigger one inside.
I opened it, and found a bigger one inside.
I opened it, and found a bigger one inside.
I opened it, and found a bigger one inside..

Billy Bang the Human Cannonball

So
yellow kite
fronts a blue sky.
Peaceful up here so tail
ribbon tied. But who's this? Only
Billy Bang the Human Cannonball! Matinee
arcing, swift scattering Billy, whiffing of cordite, got
fired again. So yellow sunbursts fleck his blue BB helmet. Tongue
tied by the beauty of flight, he goggles, singed eyelashes and kite tail
moustaches. "May lords, ladies hand gennemen. For one week
only we present *The Human Cannonball!*". Billy feels the
cold wind riffling overalls, a Las Vegas dealer working a
new deck. *FFFFTTTTTTTTTTTTTT!* Up yonder,
elemental, like a simile he clocks
the gravity of his situation.
Bye bye Billy Bang
say the swifts.
Say the
clouds.

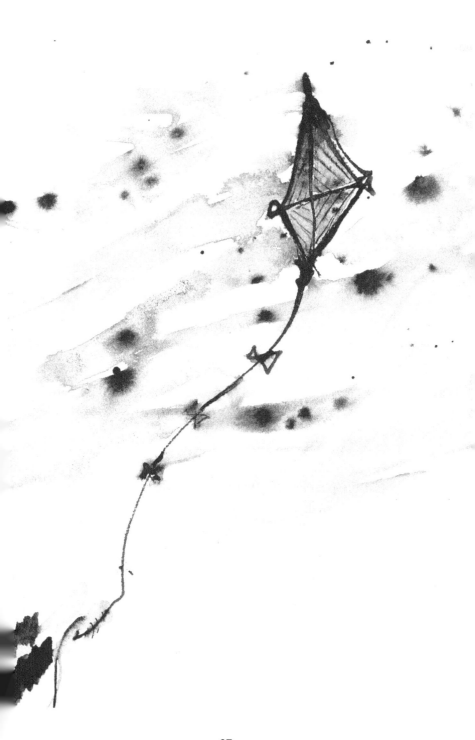

Eulogy

We are gathered here today
to remember our dear friend Chardonnay,
who passed away from some kind of attack.

In one hand a Big Mac
and in the other a shot of Tuaca,
somehow managing to pleasure Jezza, a shelf stacker
from Lidl in the loading bay
redolent of piddle.
Goods inward, as they say.

A friend to many and sadly missed,
always up for it, always pissed.
Ashes to ashes, dust to dust,
had a nob tattooed on her bust.
Deeply loved but not forgot,
on her grave, her last mug shot.

All the better to send her off in,
Lee and Jez have pimped her coffin,
in which Chardonnay rests in peace
in that place where there ain't no police.

Serendipity

A new practice manager, Dominic,
at the cosmetic vaginal clinic
with a brief to maximise resources

joins forces
with the new head honcho
in a Topshop poncho
at the budget restaurant right next door
with a mission to locally source
ingredients.

Expedient!

Bags bulbous in barbecue black
bulging with butchered bits out the back.

Serendipity!

Now when the doc has finished stitchin'
the leftovers go into the kitchen,
and the trimmings from a labiaplasty
make a lip-smackin' chicken pasty.

Simple Simon, master pieman
works his magic on a hymen.

"Ooh, I can't decide about me perineum."
"Come on love, Carpe diem.
Your vaginal rejuvenation
could become a taste sensation."

What they snip off down below
is sprinkled on the pizza dough,
and if there is a yeast infection
it makes the dough rise to perfection.

The hairy bits unidentified
become pork scratchings when deep fried.

The leftovers from that clitoral unhooding
will help bulk out the chef's black pudding.

But then the whole thing came a cropper.
Health and Safety and the coppers
took away the piles of trash
waiting to be turned to cash.

The soft pink lumps
were properly dumped.
Those remnants of discarded lips
destined to be crispy strips,
and those scraps of old vagina
are off the menu in the diner.

Politically correct hypocrisy,
self-serving smug bureaucracy,
goody-goody nanny state,
blah blah blah mortality rate.
Piggy livers and moocow hearts.
What's a few old body parts?
Maybe within us all there's hidden
an ancient taste for things forbidden.

Brisket

When I was a kid, the neighbours screamed and swore -
we heard through the wall that kept us from next door.
One day, while we were having our teas
(brisket, spuds, the usual peas,
salt and pepper, bit of mustard,
and afterwards, some pud and custard)
my dad, the better to hear the brawl,
gave us all a glass to place to the wall.
We listened, mum and dad, kids, eyes wide
to four glasses being placed to the other side.
Seems they'd tired of acting mad.
"Nosy bastards!" said me dad.

The Bitchling Deacon

This is a tale of the Bitchling Deacon.
Barefoot, dressed in canvas kilt and frock coat
as black as the devil's nutbag,
the Bitchling Deacon roves the Downs.
He leaps onto trig points and pisses a perfect circle
then blanches his face with the chalky albedo.

Only the crows knows where he goes.

Chanctonbury, Cissbury, rings are his thing.
Big and brassy, he wears them at night all naked,
when the deacon knows the Beacon is all his own.
He turns summersets, performs handstands,
his hairy balls bouncing back and forth.
Son of a bitch and a defrocked vicar,
the Bitchling Deacon is wild and fictitious,
like you and me.

Once upon a time, on a mushroom high,
he scared a man to death
and made a brew from the widow's tears.
His purple veiny bulbous drinker's nose
fits perfectly in the socket of his one-eyed girlfriend, Ursula,
who lives in the shadow of the dyke.
To Lewes Races, then, and a night of gillravage
but first to the house of his friend Don Nippery Septo.
He bangs on the door with his cane:

"Rise up, Don Nippery Septo, out of your easy degree!
Put on your sounding crackers and your down-treaders
and come and see!
Call up Dame Paradise, and your daughter Stride-a-Bush.
White-faced Simile has run up High Cockalorum
with Igniferum on her back
and without absolution we shall be all undone."

The deacon, the don and the devil's dyke girlfriend
then to the house of their friend Old Shake-a-Leg –
seven feet tall, with cloak of black and conical comical white hat.
The Bitchling Deacon bangs on the door with his cane:

Shake-a-leg, old Shake-a-Leg -
to bet upon the pony prancers,
spike the drinks of Morris dancers,
past the fires of the charcoal burners
and the barks of the teacup turners.
Shake-a-leg, old Shake-a-Leg!

At the races, the deacon puts all the gelt he doesn't have
on a filly from over the water,
and the filly would have done them a favour
if she'd stayed on the boat.
Old Shake-a-Leg chooses a thoroughbred,
but he doesn't see the word
FRAGILE
a foot high on its haunches.
In short, they lose a packet, but gain a brace of yarns,
which are priceless.

Midnight comes.
Dame Paradise and Stride-a-Bush out cold
in the brewers' yard.
Don Nippery Septo, Shake-a-Leg and Ursula skimming
flints off the backs of sheep,
while the Bitchling Deacon,
barefoot, dressed in canvas kilt and frock coat
as black as the devil's nutbag,
roves the Downs.

Only the crows knows where he goes.

Simian's Last Ride

When Lady Luck abandoned Uncle Simian
he was driving his truck
through the New Forest bound for Dagenham.

A pony ^{leapt} from nowhere,
and the truck didn't want to go
where Simian desperately steered it.
He hit a tree.

It wasn't the **Wallop** from the tree that did for Simian,
but the pallet filled with fifty packs of airbags
meeting the back of his Auntie Nells.

The airbag fitted to Simian's truck,
whose appearance he'd briefly anticipated,
stayed stubbornly un-inflated.

And now, the epitaph etched deep into the
stone which marks his grave reads
"Airbags kill more people than they save."

Strange to relate, his brother, my uncle Teo,
died the exact same date doing 70 in his Mondeo.

He had expected that beyond the sign that showed
"Motorway ends in one mile" the road
would continue in some other form.

Grappling Hooks

Recriminations flew as the
two shoplifters cluelessly
realised that there was no escape
from the revolving door
of the ZZZZips Army and Navy store.
The end of their criminal japes.
"I told you that stealing grappling hooks
was asking for trouble." John Brown said to Mary Brooks
in *vox humana*.
"I told you that stealing grappling hooks
was asking for trouble." Mary Brooks said to John Brown
in *vox celeste*.

A passing Zen master was asked by the police
to sign a witness statement. He was not released
for two hours, so was late to enter
a lecture he was giving at the Buddhist Centre.
The audience had grown tired
and started a slow one-hand clap.

Rope

My ex-wife laughed and screeched
that she didn't need to prove I was having an affair –
if she gave me enough rope, I'd hang myself.
In the event, she gave me too much rope,
so I made a macrame plant pot holder,
climbed a cliff face,
tied a sheepshank,
lassooed a calf,
made a tree swing,
moored a ship,
challenged a stranger to a tug of war,
built a bridge across a ravine,
walked a tightrope,
made a nice pair of espadrilles,
performed a rope trick,
tied a pretty girl to the railway track,
bought a fetish manual,
threaded some soap,
hung out some washing,
towed my dad's car
and skipped with some little girls.
Now I'll hang myself.

Ben Triloquist

Ben Triloquist was down on his luck. The glory days
of the Palladium and TV were far away.
There was nishta work for an ageing vent,
and what there was wasn't worth a cent.
He looked around the Queen Of The North,
a rust bucket lurching back and forth,
which was hosting a variety cruise
up the Humber (an estuary whose
description as the arsehole of England, with Hull
halfway up seemed to Ben to insult
arseholes).

*

He was bottom of the bill, propping up show biz
acts even seedier than his.
To make things worse, he was still on the mend
after an acid attack by an automatonophobic nob end
which, unusually, had left his eek
better looking than the previous week.
Figured, rather than disfigured.
Still, he was depressed.

He unpacked his puppet
from the battered leather case with the beer stains up it.
"Well looks like we've hit the bottom Mr Bailey.
You can hang up your straw capello and ukulele.
But I think before we go
there's time for one last show."

They went up on the silent deck,
the night as black as a limo wreck.
He slipped Mr Bailey onto his arm,
in his ogles a steely calm,
clambered over the safety rails
and jumped among the fishy tails.

Ben sinks, but Mr Bailey floats.
There's silence as the boat
slowly moves away.
Among the spray
Mr Bailey's orbs revolve inside his nut
several times, then open and shut.
He shouts "Helk, helk!
Throw ne a leich gelt!"
On deck, Marie
strains to hear and see,

"Did you hear something Ron?"
"No – bottle of beer anyone?"

gottle of geer
gottle of geer
gottle of geer
gottle of geer
gottle of geer
gottle of geer
gottle of geer
gottle of geer

Love Is Just a Stupid Game

Love is just a stupid game,
like Pooh Sticks on the Seine.
As autumn wore her gown
there were no sticks around,
but, abandoned by two cats (deux chats)
we found two cold and stiffened rats.
We dropped them from the pont,
but as mine edged in front,
it sank like so much lead,
and your rat streaked ahead,
so vital and alive,
and so your rat survived.
It scuttled down the lane,
yes, love is a stupid game.

Zip Took a Ladder

Zip took a ladder to an old beech tree,
and to a brawny bough he bore.
Then through that fork he sat upon
our Zip was seen to saw.
Soon there came a rifle crack
as right through the limb he hacked.
And while the branch stayed anchored there
the tree drifted high into the air,
was absorbed into the V formation
of the great beech tree migration.
Down below, Zip, open mouthed
watched the beech trees flying south.

Scrabble

They played Scrabble now and again round at Rose's bijou gaff.
Things got intense between the schlumph and the cackle.
Rose had boned up on unusual words – *mackle,*
aa, yok, ae, echm and rhaphe.

Tessa preferred to use words she knew already.
Last month they met up at Tessa's lattie
and the second word that Rose put down was *gatthi.*
Tessa was sure Rose must have learnt it specially.

The further Rose got ahead, the more irate got Tess.
However, she had bonaroo scores with *quaint* and *bevel*
until at last they were dead neck and level.
Then with her final go, Rose won with *finesse.*

Tessa peered through a swirling mist
felt as the room spin span spoon.
She threw the board across the room,
and stabbed her pen in Rose's chest,

where it quivered like an arrow.
"*Aa*" Rose said, "*Yok ae echm*", drooled
and slipped to the floor in a bloody pool
clutching feebly at the biro.

Tessa's letters drifted by the body.
U.P.P.A.N.C.E.

Mark Field's Prophecy

As a snotty kid, Mark Field
revealed
to his teacher
that in the future,
when he was a grown up, yeah,
in the future he would wear
silver clothes, see the stars
and ride around in a flying car.

"Precocious brat!"
said Miss Kitkat.

Years went by, as years they do,
and as time flies, so time it flew.
Then Mark was a grown up man,
and changed his name to Marc Bolan
(yes, it's true readers, Marc Bolan's real name was Mark Field).

His boas were feather, his hats were top,
his credit was good at the glitter shop

and his childish prophecy came true
when, Marc in silver romper suit,
driving his Mini in a shower of rain
flew through the air near Gypsy Lane
Barnes, then hit a sycamore.

He saw
stars, heard birdies twitter
before he bit the glitter
dust.

Marc wore silver clothes, saw stars
and rode in a flying car.
So be careful what you prophecy
cause it might bite you in the eye
and if you go to Barnes, maintain
a modest speed near Gypsy Lane.

Magenta

Magenta
The holistic therapist
went ballistic
when Terry pissed
on her door mat.
"Terry, you twat,"
she yelled,
"That's going to smell!"

Terry, though coarse,
was full of remorse.
To Magenta
he sent a
Hallmark card.

"With fondest regards,
sorry I pissed on your mat.
It's been a tough week what with this and that."

The manager of Hallmark was delighted
to have shifted this card which had blighted
the shelves since for ever
so he gave Trevor,
the salesman, the afternoon off.

After a bit of scoff
Trevor went to Magenta's for some reiki
but found it too flaky
and it was hard to ignore
the pissy mat smell wafting under the door.

Eve

Eve (the wife of a thief,
whose life
was curtailed
when he was impaled
on a rail)
did a double take
at the post mortem wake
when the waitress
from the caterers
served tearful drunks
with ~~sausages, cheese cubes, pineapple chunks~~
~~pickled onions~~ and ~~olives~~, all transfixed
on pointy wooden cocktail sticks.

On the bus

There's a smell of dam povercoats,
the sound of giggling girls.
A blind sawny moves down the aisle.
A couple, blind to the world,
inosculate on the back seat.
The wheels on the bus go round and round.
We are stationary, but the streets
move past
with the occasional stop.
The windows slowly melt
allowing the dam povercoat smell to exit
and the smell of bus diesel to enter.
The less-than-perfect seats lose their substance but keep their
shape,
floating like clouds across an antedeluvian landscape.
"Any more fares please?" asks the conductor from 40 years ago.
"What's a conductor, mum?" asks a kid through bubbles of snot.
"What's snot?" asks a Kyrgyz student in a dam povercoat leafing
through a 40 year old Soviet dictionary.
Girls giggle.
I press the red button and bells toll.
For whom? For me.

A Good Day in Dudley

Tarzan come to Dudley.
See woman with sad face.
Woman have banana.
Sad face but have banana!
Cheetah have banana, happy face!

Mangani people say banana like yellow smile.
Happy fruit.
Tarzan want speak to woman
but Tarzan   think   woman   think   Tarzan ..
Tarzan   think   woman   think   Tarzan ..

Tarzan strong as two lions but not good with complex grammar!
Instead, Tarzan go AAAAAAHAHAHAHA!
Woman drop banana,
run like gazelle.
But…not look sad.
Woman look alert – animated.
So… woman not sad -
Tarzan have banana -
A good day in Dudley!

The Hundred Year Old Man

The Hundred Year Old Man caught a train to the north.
He distrusts the periodic table, the Hundred Year Old Man won a fish at the fair.
The Hundred Year Old Man holds his nose open.
He shouts at the TV, the Hundred Year Old Man ran away to sea.
The Hundred Year Old Man has an acre in Kent.
He lives by the sword, the Hundred Year Old Man farts nervously.
The Hundred Year Old Man is barred from the bungery.
He watches the sun go down, the Hundred Year Old Man saw an angel in a silver robe.
The Hundred Year Old Man reads the bible – just in case.
He has big plans, the Hundred Year Old Man went down to the river.
The Hundred Year Old Man has a scar from the war.
He's not dead, just resting.

Synchronised Swimmers

We moved into our new house, which was cool
cause it came with a full sized indoor pool.
But my whole family are pants at swimming,
so I splashed out on some synchronised swimmers to put in.
They don't eat much, and the filters take their mess,
but we went on a mini break and, yes, you've guessed!

When we come back they were floating on the top.
The kids were choked – they'd given them names – Pop,
Jimmy, Ibrahim, Colin and Yogi Bear.
We buried them in the garden, and said a lickle prayer.
Anyway, that won't happen again.
Now we've got a downhill skier called Sven.
Yes, skiers are boring, and you have to wipe their snouts,
but at least you can go on a mini break without them checking out.

And the moral of this jackanory?
Pet care is fun, but sometimes gory.
Life is visceral, life is short,
love is fleeting and comes to naught.
Synchronised swimmers are just like us
and fishy is as fishy does.
Yes, synchronised swimmers are just like us
smiley, wet and fabulous.

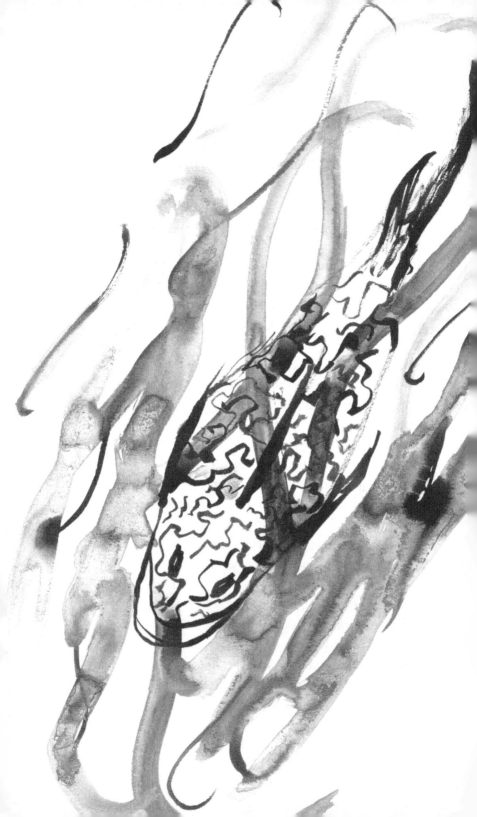

Fin

What do fish do all day?
Fish do fly aquatic, like berds.
The water their flipping beauty doth embrace
and with surround support them.
Lovely Fish. Yummy Fish.
So some time fish do caught and eaten
or eaten only
or caught only, and then returnèd waterwards
which does confuse a fish e'en to the end of its days,
hence the surprised face.
Some fish do cleave together ashoal.
Others do like to be sole.
Some denizens of the deep
are all at sea, unsure if they are-fish
or not-fish,
clams and such,
cuttlefish and the like.
Wales and their ilk make milk.
Be that as it is, moot,
they do do the same as fish do
they do sparkle wet in sunlight.
Fin.

Recipe for a Love Cake

Ingredients

1 Tablespoon of Contentment
1 Cup of Thoughtfulness
1 Cup of Encouragement
1 Pinch of Forgiveness
A dash of Faith and Trust

Lots and lots of Praise

Consideration is a must

Take love and loyalty and blend in kindness and understanding. Add friendship and surprise, stirring well. Fold in passion with an abundance of laughter. Bake with sunshine and rainbows. Garnish with patience.

Meanwhile, in a saucepan, mix together equal quantities of resentment, loathing and infidelity, and when bitter and partly congealed, pour over the love cake and leave to deteriorate for 30 or 40 years.

Best served cold.

St Mary Magdalene

Sitting on a bench
outside St Mary Magdalene
I have an unexpected window
after being chucked off a train.

Underfoot,
fag butts,
the ash of Lambert and Butler,
Benson and Hedges,
mixed up with the ashes of
Connies and Regs,
Stanleys and Veras,
assorted old geezers.
Suddenly sneezes,
red eye and wheezes.

Allergy in a country church yard.

In Canals

A doll's house,
plastic cows,
wedding vows.
Steel beams,
fish scale gleams,
broken dreams.
Prams,
tin cans,
plans.
A cushion,
pollution,
New Years' resolutions.
Traffic cones,
old mobile phones,
low towpath moans.
Baked bean tins,
potato skins,
mortal sins.
Novelty ties,
cartons of fries,
impossible lies.
Eagles cassettes,
soggy cigarettes,
bitter regrets.
Bits of armchairs,
locks of hair,
fleeting affairs.

Bags,
fags,
cold midnight shags.
Reeds,
weeds,
a woman's needs.
Packets of Pringles,
jukebox singles,
first kiss tingles.
Wedding band,
severed hand,
one-night stand.
Fishes,
dishes,
wishes.
Amazing what you find in canals.

The Butcher

His tongue out in concentration,
the butcher sews up the indentations
left by nocturnal mice
in the turkeys' meaty thighs.
The fat meaty thighs
of his meaty fat wife
Mabel
lurk under the table.

They work alone.
No words or love survive the combat zone.
The light is trying
to escape from the tripe, lying
luminously in the steel trays.
Jazz music plays
on the radio next door.

A few stitches more,
and the butcher lays down his thread
and needle, and stretches his dead
scarred, sausage hand
out into no-mans-land
to the alarm of his wife
to the arm of his wife
without tenderness. Later,
as he lies next to her
carcass on the bed,
they think with dread
of Yuletide
and homicide.

G11suspended4th

A cheery chump called Horace Cope
was happy as a lark, but
then he read in his horoscope
that to avoid getting in a rut

he should do something spontaneous.
He took a hamster and a concrete mixer
to the beach! Quite the zaniest
thing he'd ever did. Wickes'd

said it was a good 'un.
He started it and dropped the hamster in.
The little furry fella just couldn't
figure why things started to spin.

The hamster, let's call him Neal
(what with Neal being his name)
had spent some time running on wheels
but this was a new ball game.

It was awesome! Neal squealed,
went round and round,
head over hamster heels -
a rodent moment quite profound.

Horace felt his joy
and cranked the mixer up to max
sending Neal flying over the hoi polloi.
"Centrifugal force" he thought, then whacks

his head on George Harrison's banjo – CHEUNG!!
George'd been searching for the opening chord
for Hard Day's Night. "Here you go"
squeaked Neal "G11suspended4th"

Escher

As Escher got older
he bearded his wife and told her
he was finding it harder to get
up the apples in their large maisonette.
She sent off for some stairlift brochures,
arm and a leg, but they all seemed kosher
and he decided to go
for a Watchet Smoothglide 2.0.

The installation took a whole day
as he needed to get all the way
to his studio on the second floor,
and though the fitters huffed and swore
they got it done by half past three,
showed him how to work the seat,
showed him all the lift controls,
then off to the rub-a-dub dub they stole.

Tingling with ticipation
Escher prepared for embarcation.
He followed instructions to the letter
and even named the stairlift Jetta
for his wife. He cracked open some Bolly
lit a fag, and feeling jolly
got in the chair with his champagne flute
and set off on the scenic route,
watching his hallway recede from view,
like a very slow, wa-hooo,
roller coaster ride. The chair
turned onto the landing, from there
up the second flight.

Escher was not a mite
surprised to find
that having been consigned
to the very top of the stair,
he was right back where
he'd started it all,
in the ground floor hall.
He picked up the blower, sighed,
and dialled Freephone Smoothglide.

Cobblestones and Spiders' Threads

They met
in a 70's discotheque
called Hit the Deck.
It was 1991
but they weren't on
the dance floor.
She was cleaning,
he, burgling.
She wasn't fussy -
he was a biped whose thumbs were opposed.
He proposed.
He was smitten,
kitten,
bitten,
she was sooo beautiful
he wanted to write her words that soft he had to buy a
special pencil
15B.
A pencil so soft
the words lay on the page like spiders' threads.
Could only be read
in dawn light refracted through
dew.

But she was hard,
15H hard,
like cobblestones hitting a drunk off guard.

Cobblestones and spiders' threads
were never meant to go
and so
they didn't.

In Like Flynn

Errol Flynn couldn't enter a room
without hoofing the door off its hinges. POOM!
Negotiate stairs without sword waving stunt-
men reversing in front.
Hatch an idea
without slapping his thigh, dear.
Whenever there was a whiff of peril
look around and up popped Errol.

His mum, Lily, lived in Woodingdean,
and, in pursuit of her dog, who had been
a naughty boy, as doggies are,
was **hit** by an Isetta bubble car.
250ccs carry some poke.
She shouted "Goodness!" then she croaked.

Of all the fates that could have met her,
to be knocked down by an Isetta…

The driver, who shall be nameless
was, it seems, entirely blameless
and the day after he scraped Errol Flynn's ma
off the windscreen of his new bubble car,
he received an after-sale questionnaire
from Isetta customer care.
His reply was concise, almost gruff -
"Them wipers just aren't big enough".

Marelle (Lily) Flynn, mother of Errol, died in 1966 after being knocked over by a bubble car while crossing Falmer Road near her home in Woodingdean, Brighton, to retrieve her dog.

Wimbledon Legends on the Skids

Ilie Nastase sat on the karzi,
drunken bloody crawl.
Had a scratch, blew out a match
and whistled bugger all.

Monica Seles was winking at fellas
with oaths and hums and jests.
I'm telling you, sonny, she lost her money,
from out of her auld string vest.

Billy Jean King was quite the thing
in her brown paper bag.
The bag just is, and Billy just is,
and now she's on the rag.

Serena and Venus spotted a penis,
whole caboodle and kit.
Borissy Becker said "Oi that's my pecker"
and made off home with it.

John McEnroe was sat on the po
while humbugs and barnacles grew.
Evonne Goolagong said "Sing us the song
of the pope with the titty tattoo."

Arthur Ashe once grew a moustache
in the middle of his face.
A libertine then sucked it clean
like in that other place.

Andy Murray ate a curry,
huge pear in his hand.
"Me old tin kettle has lost its metal"
says Little Ferdinand.

Navratilova drove a Rover,
chrome and leatherette.
The human bees attacked her knees
and stung the Internet.

Rafa Nadal was sat in the hall
dreaming of glass decanters.
The London force had bummed his horse
"Me bonny me Tam o' the Shanter".

No Animals

The Hammond organ always sounds
like it's hurtling towards the ground
from the top of the Empire State
(with Leslie in orbit around)
swelling from a whisper to a scream at the draw of a bar
the black and white keys tumbling down
like Chet Baker's tragic teeth.

But I've carried enough of 'em
up metal fire escapes
into disinfectant dance halls
to know that if a Hammond actually falls
from the top of the Empire State
it'll hit the ground
before Jimmy McGriff could play the intro
to "I've got a woman".

No animals were injured in the writing of these words
but one man was squished on the sidewalk – splat! -
A big chord ensued – his last – be flat.

Were we go if is no love?

Unhaunted live the sun so not to wander here.
Deep and dazzle you, glide invisible,
were we go if is no love?

Dimsy glow worms face the late dusky moon.
The withered moon, eye of faded heaven
were we go if is no love?

Mouse the darkness early whisking. Light traps
the rain of summer, short and spring
were we go if is no love?

Daffy dill evensong breath. Of pride
gasping white like, sleeping wax like,
were we go if is no love?

Graffiti in Barrack Yard, Brighton